D1707959

greatest
artists

Vincent
van Gogh

Jennifer Howse

MEDIA ENHANCED BOOKS
AV2
BY WEIGL™
ADDED VALUE • AUDIO VISUAL

www.av2books.com

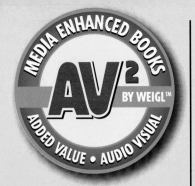

Go to **www.av2books.com**, and enter this book's unique code.

BOOK CODE

G392226

AV² by Weigl brings you media enhanced books that support active learning.

AV² provides enriched content that supplements and complements this book. Weigl's AV² books strive to create inspired learning and engage young minds in a total learning experience.

Your AV² Media Enhanced books come alive with...

Audio
Listen to sections of the book read aloud.

Key Words
Study vocabulary, and complete a matching word activity.

Video
Watch informative video clips.

Quizzes
Test your knowledge.

Embedded Weblinks
Gain additional information for research.

Slide Show
View images and captions, and prepare a presentation.

Try This!
Complete activities and hands-on experiments.

... and much, much more!

Published by AV² by Weigl
350 5ᵗʰ Avenue, 59ᵗʰ Floor
New York, NY 10118
Website: www.av2books.com

Copyright © 2017 AV² by Weigl
All rights reserved. No part of this publication may be reproduced, stored in a retrieval system, or transmitted in any form or by any means, electronic, mechanical, photocopying, recording, or otherwise, without the prior written permission of the publisher.

Library of Congress Cataloging-in-Publication Data

Names: Howse, Jennifer, author.
Title: Vincent van Gogh / Jennifer Howse.
Description: New York : AV2 by Weigl, 2016. | Series: Greatest artists |
  Includes index.
Identifiers: LCCN 2016004403 (print) | LCCN 2016005070 (ebook) | ISBN
  9781489646279 (hard cover : alk. paper) | ISBN 9781489650351 (soft cover :
  alk. paper) | ISBN 9781489646286 (Multi-user ebk.)
Subjects: LCSH: Gogh, Vincent van, 1853-1890—Juvenile literature. |
  Painters—Netherlands—Biography—Juvenile literature.
Classification: LCC ND653.G7 H69 2016 (print) | LCC ND653.G7 (ebook) | DDC
  759.9492--dc23
LC record available at http://lccn.loc.gov/2016004403

Printed in the United States of America in Brainerd, Minnesota
1 2 3 4 5 6 7 8 9 0 20 19 18 17 16

032016
210316

Editor: Heather Kissock   Art Director: Terry Paulhus

Every reasonable effort has been made to trace ownership and to obtain permission to reprint copyright material. The publishers would be pleased to have any errors or omissions brought to their attention so that they may be corrected in subsequent printings.

Weigl acknowledges Getty Images, Corbis, Alamy, and iStock as its primary image suppliers for this title.

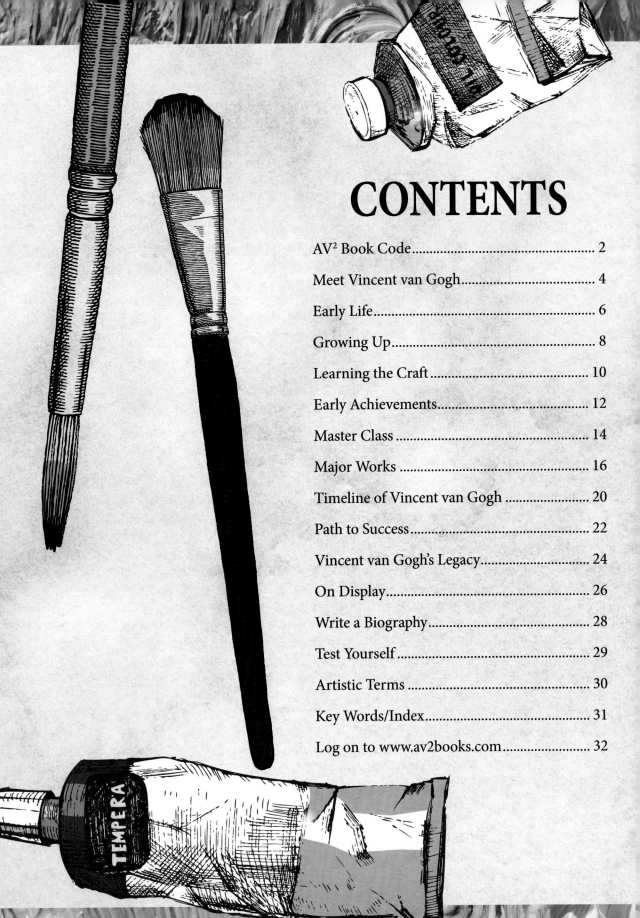

CONTENTS

Meet Vincent van Gogh

Van Gogh created almost 900 paintings over a 10-year period. This means that, on average, he produced two paintings every week.

*V*incent van Gogh was an artist who used color and **symbolism** to portray the world around him. Through his art, he provided a new approach to common scenes. To van Gogh, painting was about expressing emotion. He used colors and brushstrokes to convey his personal reaction to his subject.

Many of van Gogh's paintings portrayed scenes of nature and the farming communities of the Netherlands, Belgium, and France.

Van Gogh's style of painting was part of a new art movement called Post-Impressionism. It developed in response to another movement called Impressionism. As the name suggests, Impressionist art was based on painting an impression, or likeness, of a subject. Impressionist artists worked with color to show the effects of light and to capture a moment in time. Post-Impressionism took a step away from this approach. It focused on the use of abstract forms and patterns to portray the artist's own ideas about his or her subject. Many modern artists were influenced by van Gogh's approach to art. His paintings paved the way for the more abstract works that appeared in the 20th century.

Even though he is now considered one of the world's great master artists, van Gogh never achieved fame during his lifetime. In fact, he only sold one painting while he was alive. Since his death, however, van Gogh's paintings have been sold for some of the highest prices ever paid for artwork.

At a 2006 auction in London, England, van Gogh's *L'Arlésienne, Madame Ginoux* sold for $40 million.

Early Life

Vincent Willem van Gogh was born in Zundert, Netherlands, on March 30, 1853. His father, Theodorus, was a Protestant minister. His mother, Anna, was an artist. Vincent and his family lived in the village **parsonage**.

Theodorus and Anna had lost their first child the year before Vincent was born. They named Vincent after him. Over time, Vincent was joined by two brothers, Theo and Cornelius, and three sisters, Anna, Elisabeth, and Willemina. The van Goghs were a tight-knit family who were encouraged to support each other. Theodorus and Anna worked hard to provide their children with a good education and a proper upbringing. Attending church services, reading books, and singing were a regular part of family life. Vincent's parents believed that these activities helped strengthen the mind.

The van Gogh's Zundert home was located in the center of the village. The house itself was demolished in 1903. A museum devoted to Vincent was built in its place.

Of all his siblings, Vincent was closest to Theo. The brothers had a lifelong friendship and were devoted to each other. Many of the details of Vincent's day-to-day life are known because of the many letters he and Theo exchanged over the years.

"If you truly love nature, you will find beauty everywhere."

Vincent and Theo shared a great love of the outdoors and of nature. This enjoyment of the outdoors started at an early age, when the family would go on walks together around Zundert. As Vincent grew older, he would go for walks alone in the countryside to observe the nature around him.

Map of the Netherlands

GREAT BRITAIN

North Sea

Amsterdam ◉

. The Hague

NETHERLANDS

Zevenbergen .
Zundert . • Tilburg

London ◉

• Antwerp

Brussels ◉

BELGIUM

GERMANY

FRANCE

N

0
50 Kilometers   50 Miles

◉ Capital
● City
▨ Netherlands
☐ Other Countries
▨ Water

Growing Up

Vincent attended the local school in the village of Zundert. At the age of 11, his parents enrolled him in a boarding school in the nearby city of Zevenbergen. When he turned 13, Vincent began attending high school in the town of Tilburg. He received high grades in languages and performed well in his other subjects. However, halfway into his second year, Vincent abruptly left the school. He moved back into his parents' house and never returned to his studies.

It was in Tilburg that Vincent took his first drawing classes. At the time, the city had a population of about 20,000. Today, more than 200,000 people live there.

When Vincent was 16 years old, his uncle, also called Vincent, helped him obtain his first job. The elder Vincent worked for an international **art dealer** called Goupil & Cie. He arranged for his nephew to be hired as an **intern** at the firm. Vincent began working out of an office in the seaside city of The Hague. Four years later, the firm hired Theo as well, but he was sent to work in Brussels, Belgium. Letters between the brothers at this time describe Vincent's fascination with the art he was selling, as well as his informal education into artistic techniques and styles.

Vincent signed his paintings with his first name only.

Vincent

By the age of 20, Vincent was making more money than his father.

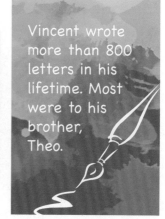

Vincent wrote more than 800 letters in his lifetime. Most were to his brother, Theo.

The National Gallery is considered one of the most prestigious art galleries in the world. It has more than 2,300 works in its collection.

In 1873, Goupil & Cie transferred Vincent to their office in London, England. When he was not working, Vincent could often be found at the British Museum and the National Gallery. Here, he studied the works of the some of world's best-known artists. He was especially drawn to paintings that portrayed the lives of peasants.

"Great things are not done by impulse, but by a series of small things brought together."

As interested in art as Vincent was, he knew he did not want to be an art dealer for the rest of his life. He spent much of his twenties trying to find a job that he liked. For a brief time, he trained to become a minister, like his father. He also worked as a teacher and a bookseller. Nothing seemed to hold his interest for long, however. It was Vincent's brother Theo who encouraged him to revisit his interest in art and pursue a career as an artist.

Anton Mauve was a celebrated Dutch artist, known for his landscapes and portrayals of rural life.

Learning the Craft

A t the age of 27, van Gogh made the decision to become an artist. He had no formal training, but began to teach himself how to draw and paint. Theo encouraged his brother and provided him with an allowance so van Gogh could focus on his art.

Van Gogh moved back to The Hague, where he began taking painting lessons from one of his cousins, an artist named Anton Mauve. Another relative, an uncle, gave van Gogh his first **commission**. He hired the budding artist to create 12 drawings of The Hague. Van Gogh welcomed the chance to practice his skills while drawing everyday scenes around the city. The commission also gave him the opportunity to learn more about perspective.

Van Gogh would often include drawings of things he had seen in his letters to Theo.

Van Gogh never married and had no children.

Often unable to afford models, van Gogh would paint self-portraits instead.
More than 30 of these self-portraits exist.

Even in his early days as an artist, van Gogh had his own style of painting. This style did not always meet with approval in the artistic community. In 1885, he enrolled at the Antwerp Academy in Belgium to learn more about painting the human form. During one lesson, two models were placed in front of the class. The

Before moving to Antwerp, van Gogh spent a year at his parents' home in Nuenen, where he set up a small studio at the back of the house.

students were told to create a painting using the models as their subjects. Van Gogh immediately began putting thick strokes of paint on his canvas. Paint dripped onto the floor as he tried to capture what he saw in front of him. His classmates were stunned. This was not how they had been taught to paint. It was not long before van Gogh left his studies at the Academy.

Antwerp is Belgium's second-largest city, after the capital city of Brussels. Even though it is seen primarily as a port city, Antwerp has been the home of several well-known artists, including 17th-century painters Peter Paul Rubens and Anthony van Dyck.

Early Achievements

In 1886, van Gogh moved in with his brother, who was now living in Paris. Theo lived in a part of the city called Montmartre, which was known for its artistic community. Here, van Gogh was able to see the work of the Impressionist painters firsthand. Colorful and full of movement, the Impressionist paintings created by artists such as Claude Monet and Camille Pissarro had a great influence on van Gogh. He also met other **innovative** artists, such as Georges Seurat and Paul Gauguin. These artists were part of a growing artistic movement called Post-Impressionism.

In preparation for his move to Paris, van Gogh arranged to study painting under Fernand Cormon, one of the city's leading historical painters. It was through Cormon that van Gogh made his initial contact with some of Paris's up-and-coming artists.

Van Gogh became fascinated with the Post-Impressionist style and began to change his own painting style as a result. He started to experiment with broken brushwork, using loose, short strokes. He also changed his **palette**. Gone were the dark, somber colors of his past works. Van Gogh now painted with the bright, vibrant colors used by the artists around him.

Gauguin was known as a rebel in the European art world. Referring to himself as a savage, he created a style of art called primitivism, which borrowed from the arts of Africa, Asia, and French Polynesia.

As with many other Post-Impressionists, van Gogh wanted to use his art as a way to express his feelings about the world around him. Symbolism became an important element in his artwork. He continued to paint landscapes, humans, and objects. However, he did not paint them as they were seen in real life. Instead, his subjects were painted in more abstract ways that had meaning to him personally.

The meaning or underlying feelings in van Gogh's paintings were expressed mostly through his use of color. He used different colors to capture a mood, whether the colors were correct for the subject or not. His use of colors could create harmony or discord, showing much more than just the physical appearance of his subject.

The view from van Gogh's Montmartre apartment became a subject for his art. He painted it on several occasions.

Master Class

*V*an Gogh lived at a time when artists were keen to apply new styles and techniques to their work. Traditional boundaries were being broken. No longer were artists trying to create an exact image of a real-life person or place. Instead, paintings were created using symbolism to express ideas and emotions. Van Gogh threw himself into learning about these new directions and applying them to his own art.

The Bodmer Oak by Claude Monet

The Barbizon School

The Barbizon school was a group of French landscape artists. Formed in the mid-19th century, the group gathered in the area around Fontainebleau Forest to paint the scenic vistas found there. Van Gogh liked the paintings of the Barbizon school because they showed him that the rural scenes and nature he loved were good subjects for paintings. The sweeping landscapes of the Barbizon artists inspired Van Gogh to master the art of landscape painting.

Japanese Woodcuts

Japanese woodcuts were a popular art form in the late 19th century. To create a woodcut, an artist would carve a pattern into a piece of wood. Colored ink would be applied to the wood. The wood would then be pressed onto another surface, like a stamp, to create a work of art. The bold outlines and contrasting colors of Japanese woodcuts inspired van Gogh and other Post-Impressionist artists. Van Gogh's painting *The Flowering Orchard* shows how he incorporated the artistry of the Japanese woodcut into his own art.

Near the Shinto Temple of Akiba by Utagawa Hiroshige

Self Portrait, 1887

Pointillism

Pointillism is a painting technique developed as part of the Post-Impressionist movement. The technique relies on using dots of paint instead of brushstrokes. When painting in the pointillist style, small dots of pure color are painted onto the canvas. The dots are placed very close together in such a way that they create a pattern or image when viewed as a whole. Van Gogh experimented with this technique in many of his paintings, including *The Restaurant de la Sirène à Asnières* and his 1887 self-portrait.

Mountains at Saint-Rémy

Impasto

Impasto is a painting technique that creates **texture**. It involves applying thick strokes of paint to the canvas. The paint is so thick that the brushstrokes are visible and the paint sticks out. Using the impasto technique allowed van Gogh to raise his paintings off the canvas into more of a three-dimensional form. His use of impasto is best seen in *Mountains at Saint-Rémy*, painted in 1889. The use of thick brushstrokes adds a dramatic intensity to the landscape. Blue is pushed through white paint to create a windy, shimmering sky.

Major Works

Van Gogh is one of the world's best-known artists. People are drawn to his use of color and the way he conveys emotion. They appreciate his ability to cast light on the lives of common folk at the turn of the 20th century. Van Gogh's unique view of the world around him has helped his art to endure and remain relevant for more than a century.

Sunflowers

Sunflowers is one of a series of paintings created during an optimistic time in van Gogh's life. He was awaiting a visit from Paul Gauguin, a painter van Gogh greatly admired. He was also planning to start an artist colony, where like-minded people could come together to create art. The bright yellows in this painting represent his optimism for the future. However, mixed in with the vibrant yellows are flowers in more muted colors. Sunflowers tend to fade quickly after being picked, so some were already dying before van Gogh could capture their brilliance. Some art lovers see this mix of bright and dull colors as a symbol of the circle of life.

DATE: 1888 **MEDIUM:** Oil on canvas **SIZE:** 36.2 × 28.7 inches (91.9 × 72.9 centimeters)

Starry Night

In *Starry Night*, van Gogh shows how the night is alive with movement and emotion. The swirling sky is filled with stars, clouds, and a bright yellow moon. The town below is bathed in moonlight. Light also shines out from windows, indicating life within the buildings. In the center of the town is the church, a sign of stability. A tall cypress tree rises on the left side of the canvas, linking the earthly world with the heavens.

Starry Night was painted while van Gogh was being treated for **depression**. The painting is said to show the view from his hospital bedroom. Even though the artist was living a tortured life at the time, *Starry Night* is considered one of his greatest works.

DATE: 1889 **MEDIUM:** Oil on canvas **SIZE:** 29 × 36.25 inches (73.7 × 92.1 cm)

The Bedroom

The simple room portrayed in *The Bedroom* was the artist's own bedroom, from when he lived in the French city of Arles. In letters to his brother, van Gogh expressed a desire to show the tranquility of the room through color. The contrasting colors work together to create the shapes, texture, and emotion of the artwork.

The painting also pays homage to Japanese woodcuts. The objects in the painting are askew, and no object throws a shadow. Van Gogh did this on purpose. He wanted to make the image appear flat, like a Japanese print.

DATE: 1888 MEDIUM: Oil on canvas SIZE: 28.3 × 35.4 inches (71.9 × 89.9 cm)

The Harvest

Van Gogh went outdoors and into a wheatfield to paint *The Harvest*. He did this because he wanted to capture the action of the harvest as it unfolded. The scene evolves in layers through the use of wavy lines and color. Harvested wheat lays across the **foreground**, while the work continues in the middle section of the painting. In the distance, a mountain range stretches across the canvas, framing the action below. While the painting is a landscape, it is also a portrayal of farming life in the 1800s. The fields are bustling with activity as men work to bring in their crops.

DATE: 1888 **MEDIUM:** Oil on canvas **SIZE:** 28.9 × 36.1 inches (73.4 x 91.7 cm)

Timeline of Vincent van Gogh

1853

Vincent van Gogh is born in Zundert, a town in the Netherlands, to Theodorus and Anna van Gogh. Theodorus is a church minister, while Anna is an artist.

1869

At the age of 16, van Gogh begins his first job, working as an intern for an art dealer in The Hague, Netherlands.

1873

Van Gogh's employer transfers him to its office in London, England. He later leaves his job as an art dealer to try other types of work, including teaching and selling books.

1880

At the suggestion of his brother Theo, van Gogh decides to become an artist, even though he has no formal training.

1886

Van Gogh moves to Paris and begins studying the works of Impressionist artists.

1888

Van Gogh moves to the town of Arles, in southern France, with plans to establish an artist colony.

1889

Van Gogh admits himself to an **asylum** in Saint-Rémy, France, to get treatment for mental illness.

1890

Van Gogh dies on July 29, with his brother Theo at his side.

Path to Success

*I*n February 1888, van Gogh moved to Arles to set up his artist colony, which he planned to call "Studio of the South." The colony was to be a place where artists could live, learn, and create together. Van Gogh invited several other artists to join him in Arles. While he waited for them to respond, he settled himself in a small yellow house and began painting the countryside. Within a month, he had completed 14 paintings.

The relationship between van Gogh and Gauguin came to an end when van Gogh sliced off a piece of his ear following an argument. Van Gogh would later paint a self-portrait showing the results of his injury.

Ultimately, only one artist answered van Gogh's call to join his colony, and that was Paul Gauguin. In October, Gauguin arrived, and the two men began painting and sharing ideas. During their time together, both artists created several works of art. However, the two men were so different in their approach to work and technique that they disagreed and fought many times. Frustrated, Gauguin left Arles after only two months.

Van Gogh was very disappointed with the way the situation had unfolded and became ill. In 1889, he also left Arles, and sought treatment at an asylum in Saint-Rémy, a village in southern France. While there, he painted some of his greatest works of art.

Theo remained supportive of his older brother throughout his troubles, and the two continued to share their experiences through letters. Van Gogh also sent his paintings to Theo, with the hope that they could be displayed and sold in the gallery where Theo worked. An opportunity arose, and van Gogh had six of his paintings included in an **exhibition** in Brussels, Belgium. An **art critic** had previously written a positive article about van Gogh's artwork, and one of the paintings, *The Red Vineyard*, was sold during the show. Van Gogh's paintings were also shown in an exhibition at the annual Salon des Indépendants, in Paris. Van Gogh was becoming known as an artist.

The Creative Process

Artists are creative people. They have vivid imaginations and are able to think in abstract ways. Still, in order to create, they must have a process, or series of steps to follow. While most artists will adapt the process to suit their individual needs, there are basic steps that all artists use to plan and create their works.

Gathering Ideas
Observing and taking inspiration from surroundings

Researching
Studying the subject or topic to determine the approach

Forming Intent
Deciding on a subject or topic to explore

Planning the Work
Obtaining the materials needed to create the work

Outlining the Project
Sketching or developing a model to follow

Creating the Work
Applying the previous stages to the creation of the final product

Making Revisions
Changing elements that are not working

Requesting Feedback
Asking for opinions from others

Completing the Work

Vincent van Gogh's Legacy

Van Gogh spent a year in treatment at the Saint-Rémy asylum, working to overcome the mental illness that engulfed him. Upon his release in May 1890, he moved to the village of Auvers-sur-Oise so that he could be closer to his brother Theo, who was still living in Paris. In Auvers-sur-Oise, van Gogh found new artistic inspiration. The village was surrounded by farms and gardens. Van Gogh spent much of his days exploring the countryside and finding new vistas to paint. He was able to create a new painting almost every day. Sadly, after just two months, van Gogh died of a self-inflicted gunshot wound.

Many of the communities where van Gogh lived have erected statues in his memory. One of the best known can be seen in Saint-Rémy.

To honor his brother, Theo arranged a memorial exhibit of his brother's work. Unfortunately, only seven months later, Theo also died. The friendship of the two brothers and their thoughts and life experiences are all recorded in the hundreds of letters they exchanged.

While living in Auvers-sur-Oise, van Gogh rented a room in the Ravoux Inn, which was owned by Arthur Ravoux. Most of the details about van Gogh's final days come from Ravoux's daughter, Adeline.

Johanna was born into a family with strong artistic connections. She married Theo in April 1889. The couple had one son, named Vincent Willem after his artist uncle.

Following the death of her husband, Theo's widow, Johanna, moved to Amsterdam and began to show people her brother-in-law's art. She loaned paintings out to museums around the world and published the letters that the brothers had shared. In 1914, Johanna had the body of Theo moved to the grave beside Vincent, in Auvers-sur-Oise.

Throughout his life, van Gogh worked very hard to learn and master his art. He created more than 850 paintings and close to 1,100 works on paper. Each work of art demonstrates his dedication to employing new techniques and styles to achieve his vision. Van Gogh's work is treasured for its contribution to the Post-Impressionist movement.

Over the years, paintings have surfaced that have been attributed to van Gogh. One of the most recent was *The Protestant Barn*. Studies continue to determine if he painted the work.

On Display

Van Gogh was a leader of the Post-Impressionist movement. As such, his wonderfully expressive paintings and drawings are an important part of art history. Van Gogh's artworks can be found in art galleries and museums around the world, where they continue to inspire artists and art lovers alike.

Van Gogh Museum

In 1925, Theo's widow Johanna died. Van Gogh's art collection was passed on to his nephew, Vincent Willem van Gogh. He loaned the art to the Stedelijk Museum in Amsterdam. However, Willem's dream was to have his uncle's art displayed in a venue of its own. He worked toward this goal for many years. Finally, in 1973, the Van Gogh Museum was opened to the public. Also located in Amsterdam, this museum has the largest collection of van Gogh's artwork in the world, with approximately 200 paintings and 500 drawings. Its holdings also include about 700 of his letters. Each year, more than 1 million people visit the museum to see the collection and to learn more about van Gogh's art and his life.

In 1999, the Van Gogh Museum increased in size with the construction of its Kurokawa Wing. Today, the wing is connected to the main building by a glass entranceway.

The Metropolitan Museum of Art is located on a part of Fifth Avenue called Museum Mile. This stretch of street features some of the city's best-known museums and art galleries.

Metropolitan Museum of Art

New York's Metropolitan Museum of Art is one of the largest art museums in the world. It was founded in 1870, after a group of influential Americans felt it was time for the United States to have a world-class art venue. Over the course of its history, the Metropolitan Museum of Art has worked to develop its collection. Today, it has more than 2 million works, ranging from a Roman sarcophagus to approximately 2,500 European paintings. The Metropolitan Museum of Art has 24 of van Gogh's works in its collection, as well as several of his letters to Theo.

Musée d'Orsay

The Musée d'Orsay is located in one of Paris's former train stations. It opened to the public in 1986, with a mission to "show the great diversity of artistic creation in the western world between 1848 and 1914." Today, it houses one of the world's largest collections of Impressionist and Post-Impressionist art. Van Gogh's works are an important part of this collection, with the Musée d'Orsay in possession of some of his best-known works. These include *The Bedroom*, *The Restaurant de la Sirène à Asnières*, and *Self-Portrait*, a painting he completed in 1889 while still living in Saint-Rémy.

The Musée d'Orsay has three different levels, consisting of the main ground floor, a series of terraces, and the top floor, which is situated above the lobby.

Write a Biography

All of the parts of a biography work together to tell the story of a person's life. Find out how these elements come together by writing a biography. Begin by choosing a person whose story fascinates you. You will have to research the person's life by using library books and reliable websites. You can also email the person or write him or her a letter. The person might agree to answer your questions directly.

Use the chart below to guide you in writing the biography. Answer each of the questions listed using the information you have gathered. Each heading in the chart will form an important part of the person's story.

Parts of a Biography

Early Life
Where and when was the person born?
What is known about the person's family and friends?
Did the person grow up in unusual circumstances?

Growing Up
Who had the most influence on the person?
Did he or she receive assistance from others?
Did the person have a positive attitude?

Developing Skills
What was the person's education?
What was the person's first job or work experience?
What obstacles did the person overcome?

Early Achievements
What was the person's most important early success?
What processes does this person use in his or her work?
Which of the person's traits were most helpful in his or her work?

Leaving a Legacy
Has the person received awards or recognition for accomplishments?
What is the person's life's work?
How have the person's accomplishments served others?

Test Yourself

1

In what country was van Gogh born?

Van Gogh was born in the Netherlands.

2

How many letters did van Gogh write in his lifetime?

Van Gogh wrote more than 800 letters in his lifetime.

3

What technique did van Gogh use to give his paintings texture?

The technique that van Gogh used to create texture is called impasto.

4

What was the name of the artistic movement that van Gogh experienced when he first moved to Paris?

While in Paris, van Gogh saw paintings in a style called Impressionism.

5

In which city is the Van Gogh Museum located?

The Van Gogh Museum is located in Amsterdam.

6

At what age did van Gogh decide to become an artist?

Van Gogh was 27 when he decided to become an artist.

7

Which museums did van Gogh like to visit when he lived in London?

While living in London, van Gogh liked to visit the British Museum and the National Gallery.

8

How many sisters and brothers did van Gogh have?

Van Gogh had two brothers and three sisters.

9

What was the name of the art dealership that gave van Gogh his first job?

Van Gogh's first job was at Goupil & Cie.

10

Approximately how many paintings did van Gogh produce in his lifetime?

Van Gogh produced more than 850 paintings over the course of his career.

Artistic Terms

The study and practice of art comes with its own language. Understanding some common art terms will help you to discuss your ideas about art.

abstract: based on ideas rather than reality

brushwork: the way an artist applies paint with a brush

canvas: cotton or linen cloth used as a surface for painting

ceramics: articles made from clay that has been hardened by heat

composition: the arrangement of the individual elements within a work of art so that they make a unified whole

easel: a folding stand used to hold up a painting while the artist is working

engraving: a print made from an image cut into wood or metal

etching: prints made from images drawn with acid-resistant material on a metal plate

form: the shape or structure of an object

gallery: a place where works of art are exhibited

medium: the material used to create a work of art

mood: the state of mind or emotion a painting evokes

movement: a stylistic trend followed by a group of artists

permanent collection: a collection of art owned by a museum or gallery

perspective: a technique used by artists to show space

pigment: fine powder that produces color; when mixed with oil or water, it becomes paint

primary color: any of a group of colors from which all other colors can be obtained by mixing

proportion: the appropriate relation of parts to each other or to the whole artwork

space: the feeling of depth in a work of art

studio: a space, room, or building in which an artist works

Key Words

art critic: a person who publishes or broadcasts his or her opinions about art

art dealer: a person or company that buys and sells art

asylum: a place for the care of people who are mentally ill

commission: the hiring and payment for the creation of a piece of art

depression: a medical condition that causes a person to feel sad and to lose interest in life

exhibition: a public display of the works of artists

foreground: the part of a view closest to the audience

innovative: new and inventive

intern: a trainee who works at a job to gain experience

palette: the range of colors used by an artist in making a work of art

parsonage: a house provided for a member of the clergy

sketching: creating a rough drawing to help in planning the final picture

symbolism: the practice of using one thing to represent another

texture: the surface quality of an artwork and how it feels when touched

Index

Log on to www.av2books.com

AV[2] by Weigl brings you media enhanced books that support active learning. Go to www.av2books.com, and enter the special code found on page 2 of this book. You will gain access to enriched and enhanced content that supplements and complements this book. Content includes video, audio, weblinks, quizzes, a slide show, and activities.

AV[2] Online Navigation

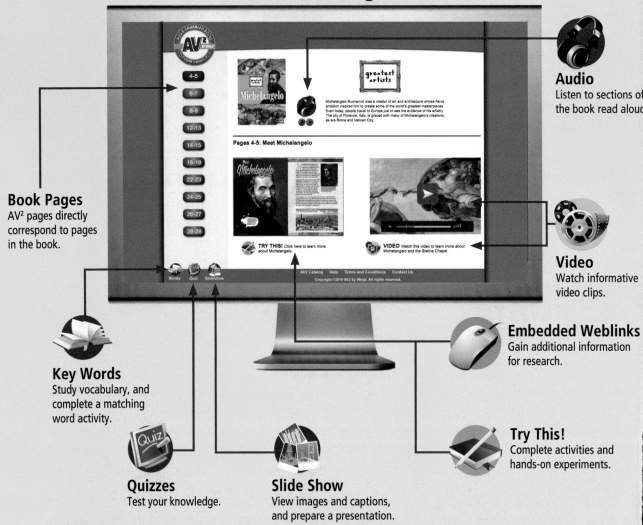

Book Pages
AV[2] pages directly correspond to pages in the book.

Audio
Listen to sections of the book read aloud

Video
Watch informative video clips.

Key Words
Study vocabulary, and complete a matching word activity.

Embedded Weblinks
Gain additional information for research.

Quizzes
Test your knowledge.

Slide Show
View images and captions, and prepare a presentation.

Try This!
Complete activities and hands-on experiments.

AV[2] was built to bridge the gap between print and digital. We encourage you to tell us what you like and what you want to see in the future.

Sign up to be an AV[2] Ambassador at www.av2books.com/ambassador.

Due to the dynamic nature of the Internet, some of the URLs and activities provided as part of AV[2] by Weigl may have changed or ceased to exist. AV[2] by Weigl accepts no responsibility for any such changes. All media enhanced books are regularly monitored to update addresses and sites in a timely manner. Contact AV[2] by Weigl at 1-866-649-3445 or av2books@weigl.com with any questions, comments, or feedback.